The Ascendant

The Ascendant

Maria Zajkowski

PUNCHER & WATTMANN

First published in 2015
Published by Puncher and Wattmann
PO Box 441
Glebe NSW 2037
http://www.puncherandwattmann.com
puncherandwattmann@bigpond.com

National Library of Australia
Cataloguing-in-Publication entry:

Zajkowski, Maria
The Ascendant

ISBN 9781922186607
I. Title.
A821.3

Cover design by Tim Cronin
Cover image 'you can do anything if you do it with confidence' by Liz Racz
Printed by McPhersons Printing Group

This project has been assisted by the Australian Government through the Australia Council, its arts funding and advisory body.

Australian Government

Australia Council
for the Arts

Contents

'My world is clear I sleep I lie in my enclosure
here in my assigned place between feet and hair and darkness
assigned to sleep and phases of identity. I am an object.

They say that in bed you learn to die'
— *Inger Christensen*

The beginning and

by the last tree in the last summer
on the hill where the last sun falls
on the things that at last mean

we are finally unwound
from the hollow arrow
around which we have spun
our ignorant lives

we leave the first last
to wait inside the darkness
where the black snow falls
like the last bird

Every tiny arrow

every tiny arrow
every arrow word

nowhere is there any thing
to be what we come after

prepare the boats for high ground
the animal of you

the first third of the end
is simple

it comes in a shower
of precise downfalls

Underland

I have been buried turning away
because you haven't understood
to draw inside this tomb
is the only life to make

All that is written is blank

all that is blank
is written at dawn

a palm to a path
a scattering of bones

your selves lost in the tracks
of one gone animal

a mist of explanations
calls this new dark home

where a stupid mind
got stuck on your tongue

you and the thought you could
better the affliction with

the sound (what is) the sound
of something the heart would have done

Fifteen griefs

it came

the hole in holiness

the final birds
I closed my eyes

lying to your disappointment

what can we do with what we can do now

a drought walked and you were sure of angels

going through your pockets for the same emptiness

as exactly one lifetime is accrued but nothing is accurate
let's be precise

sport is the word you use when nothing else describes what was lost

I worked and I worked and I worked at something surely

waiting is a fact to rain

they found me on the floor
two days after I was born again

a rock overwhelms the silence it makes

the day before is always unfinished

as if life depends
(on things)

Those things

what are those things you are
by the grave of last impressions
the bird that can't cry
though there is no now like now

those things you tied together
in the last single hour
with that musty clock
and the tapping of some god's
finger on your head
enough to break a petal from its neck

that thing you carried
the cage with a need for only you
when you opened it
a black sleep dripped on my pillow

its poison stopped the little hand
that hammered on the door
it was blood shut for a dreamy carriage
a marathon of absence

consequences became you
and I held my hands each day
until the flowers died
I ate the mountains I climbed
with no tongue on which to place
the flags of my conquest
the miracles melted in my jaw

what are those things you become
away from this and always
with your skin in a bag
and your heart no longer a heart
we meet between the wheels
alive and not alive
where there is nothing to give
that cannot be dead and beautiful tied

Surely

surely
death is an expensive
exquisite dilemma
a beautiful exhalation
to find out now

and now is for morons
who reach in the dark
and touch each other's disappointment

now we get silence
from watching knives
rise to fill the sky
our trying makes stars
aim for these lives

The higher order

we are in love again
the exits are covered with entries
and what goes in alone comes out with a hand on fire

the future exists again
where for every excuse we make
is the tree under which we were excused

again we have again
the knife cuts into the same conversation
like last night into tomorrow

so again we are at an end
the legs of morning are close round your hips
and one breath sacrifices itself for

as again we ride into sunrise
through the difficult scar
of the archangel

and again we are deceived
by what is new on the horizon
though there are new horizons in every second step

it is once again the truth
that the unseen stranger will walk
around with a strangeness in her open arms

yes again we do not talk
like the time we talked in darkness
no we cannot talk in darkness like we can talk now

The samurai

The samurai telephones in the dark,
she says the night broke in her head
and there is no valley anymore
between inside and out,
There is no river down which to float,
from the place of words
or the other pleasures,
She says there is nowhere to go,
that she is the stone
of the departed flow
and it really is that much, that cold,
the pressure of light that makes
so much dark the purpose,
She writes me a letter before it is over
and this is the boat that would sink
with our swords.

S.O.S

for …

On your back the destination
you walk all your life toward,
taking the moraines
and crevasse after bleeding crevasse,
in this deep space
(dot dot dot, dash dash dash, dot dot dot)
your eye has the faraway mountain
of silent rain,
your vision hand
holds each thing in its place
and a slow wandering herder waits
for you to come back
to yourself, the palace determined.

The goat and the reason

life becomes a fable again
the goat sits down with the lamb

the cousin marries at last
and we are not the wanderers

in this crossing a danger smiles
a couple is no other woman

be difficult for it and don't
the truth is a hole in the rain

for a thousand years
we kept a prophet for breakfast

spooning through the have-nots
to make reasons for ourselves

The four things I learned from you and how I got about it

being a real wife of masses
like most slaves are
such as days are slave to their name
and as a square holds out a hole

in this legend we have no hero
the bricks of our prison are pure light
trees on the border who helped us escape
are now together us

superstition is form
on the back of your hand
what future you preyed for is dying
to make this beautiful border

yes further to truth is what happens
I hate you I hate you
says someone in love
through the mouth of a bird

and the foot that disturbs peace
is the root caught breaking
pulling its beard with precipitation
lying to us

four futures ago we came
running from the ground and out
holding tongues without sunlight
after more future we tired

forests ignite
cairns and ablutions
fourteen thousand of you
eruptions lit with glass and moon
and the little angels who work so hard

new old has dried up
and songs of snails
dream in your ears when you are running
from sleep to sleeping

stars fall down
and you never learn
a knock at the door
means you're already in

The powerful owl

The powerful owl,
the candle in the fern,
the music in the grain,
because we have spiders
ready to bloom
I am waiting this spring
for explosions,
our myth of love in the glade
to reveal its flowers,
to drink the honey you threaten
as it rains and rains on that sun,
your hand passes through mine,
each step is each step,
the owl flies into itself.

Theories of unity

listen to the end
propped with sticks
and pierced with pointlessness

no wonder the leopard
blends nothing in
he comes for the way to leave

the smaller mountain forgives
the larger flight of death

The (un)wound

the place we kiss
has no right here

a broken spear is two
if you let them

(one hand for each
end of the struggle)

in one long melt
you lie

where no body can have comfort
a planet content

with an unknown lion
is the end of a planet

its shaken head
its walk away

how you stand is upon your self
and only half of life

Where Chiron goes

the opportunity waves goodbye
from this one single healing
which of course requires
nowhere and is nothing
but a change in the humid heart
where no future is happier
or could care less
than the one we planned to fence

The fence is gone

The fence is gone,
we are starting to see
our nudity through the branches,
the pumping berries
pinned to our hearts,

I've forgotten if you are me
or I'm you.
We switched bags somewhere.
I have to rummage through
the palings in the yard
for the knothole that used to
show me how to see the world.

I can't frame you in it now
or detect from these piles
of decrepit fence what was
so important that for so long
it needed to be kept in.

Bison grass

The time ran through
your hands like a gold snake
and you said it as though
you'd drunk it head first.
What followed is the way
you now writhe and writhe
with the memory of that
sun-wet day in your eyes,
through your words it is pouring
one hundred per cent proof
that you had a god out in that field,
you had found yourself
walking on water,
bobbing above a timeless current
in a river of bison grass.

The blue road

The blue road sings
like a leopard
wanting to be you,
There is peace in your protection
and peace in the fist
that contains all
worlds and things that we cannot,
...understand this
when we set out, our feet were silver
and now, when we are tracked
they look for some impression
I forget to give,
I care little now the song has stopped,
we were family for a while,
how did that feel
when you were a note
on the horizon screaming,
what was it like to be us
and the other thing acquainted,
truth wrong and a forgotten
independence, truth concerned with
itself and the other imperfections.

It must have a name

learning to light the rain
with my eyes
I touch the wall of things
a chasm lifts a mountain

the drop of every bruise
beyond my heart
it is a wound to let a wound
fall unheard

The problem is

trees like us
are already dead

I am left on your own
where we are all in

but you are not the thing
you so want to be

you repeat what you are
and send your self down

where trees like us
are not reached

that same head
will get you no higher

or in far enough
to solve this life

Love is a selfish life

for the purpose of travel
in an unowned body

and a view of the stars
from the stars

the form I can't contain
contains all of you

a prize plan
I climb from and into

love is a selfish life
a furniture expressed
by a self-important orbit

a space for leaves
letters
masterpieces of sunlight

a corner made from a straight line
and every reliable loss

No word

there is no word from the trees
it's sixteen weeks since we buried you
and the watching is just comfort for now

citizens of grass
we look across the same empty attachment
that yet another army of desire fails to pin down

the dead trees continue to reach for never
if you remember the privilege of the curse
that we are still here

How many cats are you

your Zen is the new me
I aspire to be as still as your death
without it,

there is nothing but nothing,
even desire causes no pain
uneven desire is beautiful
where we fade,

there my angel digs a hole
to fill a hole
out of bounds, the stars
and the star-struck

wade in and out,
the night is alone and humble alone,
small footsteps arrive

somewhere else
and here is nothing
but nothing but.

The free state

the proof of my existence
is tax deductible
so surely I would want
a percentage of each rain

a quarter of what I see
goes to the government
think not of what a mountain owes
big debts are depressing

seventy per cent of me is you
the rest is gone again
to the free state
unaccounted for

We are all critics of bread

sunsets that cannot deliver
what we last promised ourselves
and the faulty trinkets
we threw to each other
kindly indigestible,
real meat (joy) and scales,

your skin and the soufflé
that must not be disturbed,
oh to break that crust,
to roll with it, to be content
with the contents is such a charm,

and you tousled,
you undeliverable,
your magic standing
the mountain down,
your profile with the falcon
and the lioness returning.

It becomes hot, it freezes

After your new leaves arrived
mostly on a Sunday
crows kept sitting on the one
piece of time that would not go away,

huge cocoons in the trees
clutched expectation, would we reform?

Remember the daisies
we cut in your last dream
still wilt on your tongue,
not even fresh water revives a murder.

I keep killing
I keep the garden intact
if you faded to this

every river and every day
I climb down for the black
unshifting stones
you threw from your eyes.

We look at each other

everyone in the world can
by the sorrowful river
interpret the unconscious
swallow of a heart

descend to the shore
and wave ourselves goodbye
god is not a door
in our mouths

tonight the sky is better
to give than to receive

The world on hands

tonight weight
and the last thing we dropped over the edge
have found the flashing lights
of the beginning

coming down the hallway of IT
we get lost between one step
and its sister

there are walls for walls
and a rattling all night long
that makes you feel
the thing you really paid for

The rising

the comfort farmer
has hoisted you too high
and there in the light
of something that does not exist
you shine and throw
yourself into hopeless rivers
to find a fortune
cold on your plate

once the moon had feet
and walked every day
now it has learned to fly
and won't even eat
watching as we go through doors
as if one side of ourselves
was not like the other
and who can see anyway
beyond the evidence rising

Through the night wave

a hand becomes every hand
a hole becomes a home
a place to forget
the ascendant has left
a face in the dark
is what it faces
the glass forest
in all of your lives
the rope around
day and night
into death I am
repeating the unsayable

Autumn letters

Morning's corpse, its crow in the house,
in need of tuning, a chore, a buffing,
an offering to go for a walk, shoulder
the autumn written in letter after letter
of unsent sighs. Those letters, dissolving
like the afterbirds, the body that inhabits
the song, there after the echo has returned
to find it gone, a soiled space where no purity
can walk free, where the space inside
bows down, taking the body as a hood,
an echo of zero, a hearse for your words.

This is not the silence I imagined
(an approximate value)

rain
the nothing everywhere
the count of my heart is more out of being less

today is the tunnel
but nothing can find what it was
listening to the road that wants to end

the floor of the hall of the house where you lay
hands in my head and a head in my hands
the small rescue I can't decide if I performed

for you the house remains what we thought
half of the truth is gone as always
like the soul's evaporations

the immeasurable so precise tonight
your old shape takes up all that nothing
shaving light from the proof

the soundtrack plays down
you were a body
you were it

The fox suite

Walking backwards under a stick
carrying my little fox,
our fur is lifeless, silent
and you are barely warm
in my failing. I am sorry
we must do this like this
but I am not the one doing it.

I wait for you, it's your translucence
I follow with this piece of string
into and out of this mirror where
nothing lasts, with you my companion,
my little gold fox so tired,
it's our selves to cross,
our night, in glass.

* * *

The birds prefer
their heads and toes in water,
their song to be the only song
underground, what they forget
in snow is the night
breath of the fox running
and tears at the feet of the grass.
Why is so long so long and never,
that sun crashes all over us
as though *we* are the obstacle.
I prefer you, and may as well,

if we are to go around our lives
rather than through them.

* * *

Blood fox,
your music woke me
from my bellows, my ins
and the out, my daily contralto
of sad and subtle endings.
How the wind howls
for what it can't be with.
Will I know you are gone
any more than I do,
and with what harmony
can I run away
from the crying crying night.

Is nothing in death

life gives death a forest
empty of the infinite rustle
of the birds we no longer make

the wolf was never here
and faith in numbers (which are stone)
strikes from the sky

everything comes when it rains
every thing is upheld by mud
and the love we make with progress

arrows tacks blood berries
everything has flown back into dew
stars drawn to sun underground

A compass after life

when do the stems turn black
when is the crocus waiting

it is all ways this again
inside the purpose of landfall

enter the ringing meadow
the far sun pretends

lying in the joke that breathes
past thought's prison

the small sound of a world
leaving your mouth

its colour turning back
into the death you made

enter again a life
or keep the flower you lost

The white butterfly

The white butterfly is
the brown butterfly
who is the moth,
the moth is the tree
the tree is its mother
the mother is the sun
and the sun is the white
butterfly falling into every
crack, looking for a place
to hide her child.

The use of regular forms

distinguished is no format

to care is to form

hunger forms the silence

and silence is not fulfilled

the use of forms is what we thought we had use of

people say stars form

but some things are too late

wine is not really wine

but breath that forms to unform

in the new night in a form of new sleep

a hat is a form of goodbye

a hole forms where there was no hole

it is used like many things

and many things are gone

Signs of life

there is always a photograph
there is always a tiger
an apple not famous
like apricots

the ash on your head
the sky on your head
the roar of space
we are all sinking

a rose is a door
a rose is sun death
the evening of dead roses
a tiger swims in

Are we death

are we death now
can we hope at last
that this blue morning has become us
finally is there nothing to believe
coming after us
placing its steps in ours through the dew
free of the urging heart
free of the curse of hair and eyes
are we at last on the mountain
we have so long been under
the tunnel that was a song
is it over
the irritability of being ourselves
the plain fact of being dumb
are we at last over it
can we now be final
final like memory
final like stars
final like mornings
all over again

Worth repeating

thank you bird
you are the thank you bird
a curtain of birds
a modesty of birds
a skeleton of skeletons
worth repeating

the past is a beautiful fantasy
where we sat and ate lunch
pointing the amazing
out of the picture

yes it was a big day
we ended without fingers
the smell of you ran
the taste of your flight

entry to the truth
tonight is by bison
so take your position
on the back of its execution

Summer

This summer is broken,
what a poor vulture I have become,
what a cloud, what a sun
and just like you always
you're drowning again,

so I compromise,
I'll resurface in your
unfinished business if
that's where summers matter,
a fig and a peach now
the fig and *the* peach,

which summer was *just* a summer
and which death was only a death?
The sun sets on a dry sea,
a shore doubts
it was ever touched.

Many worlds are silently confused

jane joritz-nagakawa

if you are answering the question
nightly all the time
to make the wind stop
and the eagle sudden

where do you go in the dark
with sound's eye on

talking to the only thing
discovered in that last
patch of the free woods

Bodyofevidence

if there is perfection
it would be in the place we stand
why am I looking for you

underneath the fire in our sleep
dead as it lives
is it what we can't be without

I do not want your eyes
or any of those incomplete things
my ghost has after all passed
the test of you

I.M.

I'm in love's love
on this little river

the path falls behind
the ungentle death

the first following angel
floats us to her

how do I wear a cure
or swallow the stone
of living enough

the moon that drops
from my tongue is no good
I can't keep a light alone

What we began

when we began we began
I sent myself back but we never
did look into that cloud

there is too much desire to forget
what a waste we can and can't be

tonight apart looks like
what won't be itself in the light

Surviving death

Every day, surviving death, we send out our horses.
They don't come back.

Here the dry river's a place not to camp,
the night a place not to be.

An army gathers rattling its pans, thinking of home,
an army that will turn your head

to a fire in the sand where those
who've survived this wait out of time

in the dust and the gold,
with the horse you thought was gone.

The one who went away

I turn the stone in my head,
there is your room and there on the bed you sit
in a light that does not shift

you rise and rise again, never noticing
the dust or the room or the way I keep coming
though never coming in.

A stone cannot be moved from itself
and the light comes from a time without hours.

Perhaps you are the one who went away
and it was I who waited in that room
high above the expectations of ordinary days.

The dead violin

This is the past,
we are still waiting for it
The past fact and the future fact

we are in perfect symmetry,
two hundred years, days, minutes
just as absolute

this delicacy
crushes breath and releases
tiny movements of soul,
I was alive
I will be alive.

Since yesterday I spoke

I rode the rapids
I lived you and I
folded into the desert
flying the long circle

under our selves
this one horse freedom
brought down from god
for the other lunatics

here is the thing
you can't help yourself through
trading with stars
looking at maps

that are not proof
truth walks but where
your shadow is the bridge
we hear so much about

The last beautiful sweet days

The last beautiful sweet days
the red coat I wore
in the distance each time
you got up and sat down,
the undiscovered words
and another day in the jungle,
the place where and soon not the place,
the incomplete horses
the unknown clothes waiting
we go into the wrong rooms,
how do we know our lives.

Epilogue

The loophole, or, how the sky ignores us

we watch you
through the loophole
where the meaning seeps away

we never make it to the page
but pages are still missing

you became the animal
we thought thought

you sang in silence and grew so tall
your first light above the horizon

the last known unknown
we can be certain of